17 Placoderms

EVERYONE SHOULD KNOW ABOUT

STANTON F. FINK

VOLUME IX OF STANTON'S COLORING BOOKS

Acknowledgments
and Dedication

To my father, in whose books I discovered my first monsters.

To Professor Matt Friedman, who has been an enormous help with my paleoichthyological research.

To Professor John A. Long, whose books on paleoichthyology have been, collectively a ginormous lighthouse of Alexandria-like beacon for my research.

To Doctor David Morafka, who helped teach me to be more picky with my information.

To my friends, who helped push me to make this.

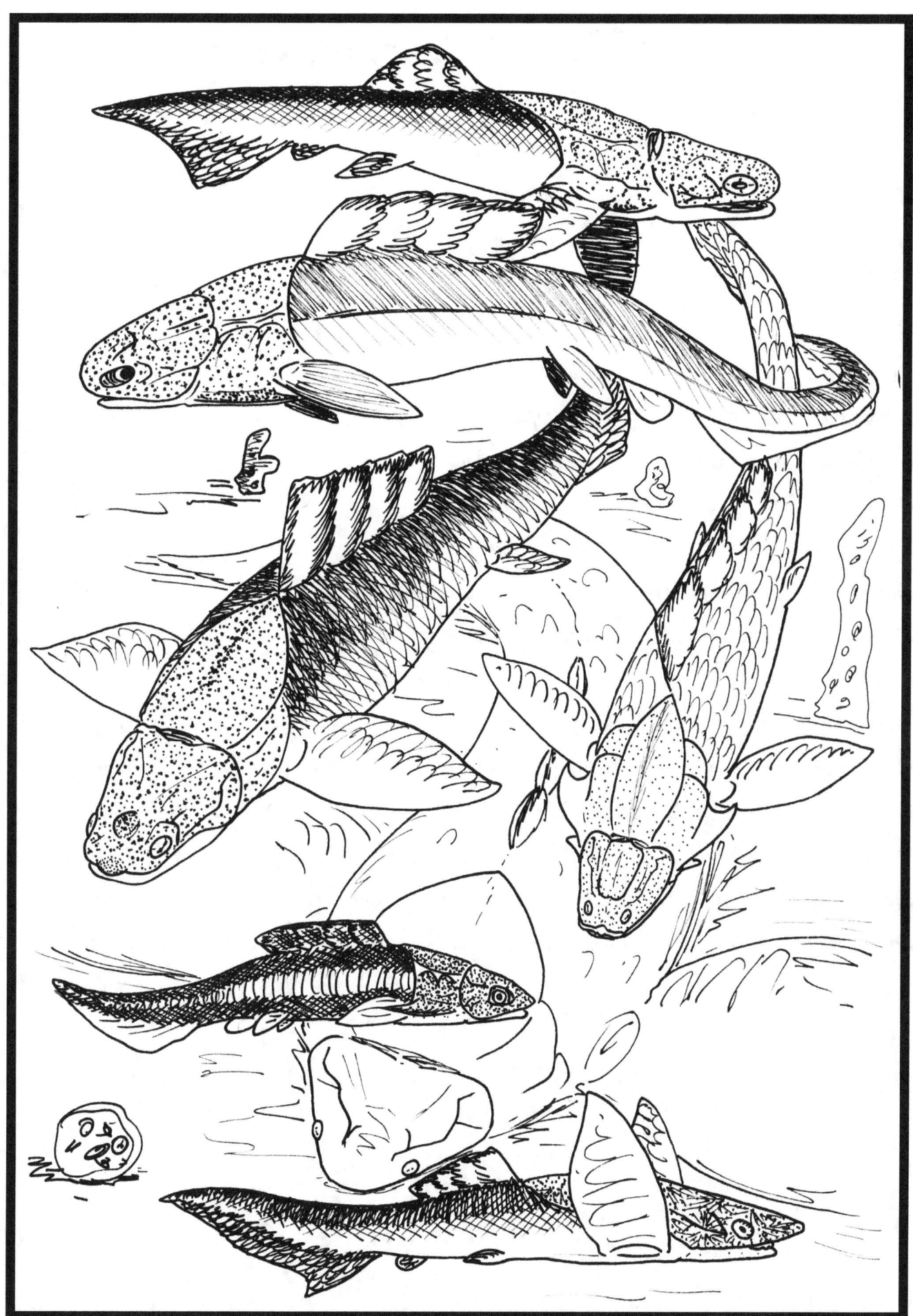

Table of Contents

Introduction

The Placodermi (or simply "placoderms") are a group of primitive gnathostome vertebrates that either are the ancestors of all other gnathostome vertebrates, or share a common ancestor with all other gnathostome vertebrates (i.e., "one's great grandfather" versus "one's great granduncle").

According to the internal anatomy of various skulls, the placoderms' closest relatives outside of Gnathostomata are the agnathans of Monorhina, including the Osteostracans (including *Cephalaspis*, *Thyestes*, etc), *Pituriaspis*, and the Galeaspids (such as *Sinogaleaspis*, *Dunyu*, etc). Placoderms are thought to have diverged from the monorhinids during or before the Early Silurian, and eventually went on to either dominate, or at least establish a presence in all known aquatic environments by the start of the Devonian Period.

When humans first began studying placoderm fossils during the 1800's, they thought these animals were sluggish bottom-dwellers, largely irrelevant footnotes of evolution who were easily vanquished by the "superior" sharks and bony fishes who were not weighted down with antiquated armor. Now that we have had almost two centuries' worth of additional information about placoderms, we humans now understand them to be important components of the Devonian ecosystems, as well as being a collective window which shows us what the first jawed vertebrates were like. The placoderms' demise now thought to have been a complex situation of them slowly dying off due to a series of environmental catastrophes during the Late Devonian, first being a pair of low oxygen periods during the Kellwasser Event between the Frasnian and Famennian Epochs, and then an even worse low oxygen even during the Hangenberg Event during the transition between the Devonian and Carboniferous Periods.

Glossary

- **Aquatic**- Living in water.
- **Arthropod**- Any member of the animal phylum Arthropoda, including trilobites, arachnids, crustaceans, insects, myriapods and their relatives. All arthropods have armor-like, jointed exoskeletons made of chitin-derived plates, sometimes reinforced with calcium carbonate, and jointed limbs.
- **Cambrian**- A period of time in the Paleozoic Era from 541 to 485 million years ago.
- **Carboniferous**- A period of time in the Paleozoic Era from 359 to 300 million years ago.
- **Cenozoic**- An era of time in the Phanerozoic Eon from 65 million years ago until now.
- **Chordate**- Any member of the animal phylum Chordata, including sea squirts, lancet fish, and vertebrates (such as lampreys, sharks, tuna, frogs, lizards, chickens, and people). All chordates have, at least at some point in their life cycle, a notochord, a long, flexible rod, usually made of cartilage, or, in the case of most vertebrates, cartilage and bone, running down the back from head to tail, directly beneath the neural tube.
- **Devonian**- A period of time in the Paleozoic Era from 414 to 360 million years ago.
- **Fauna**- In an ecological context, "fauna" refers to the animal components of an ecosystem.
- **Formation**- In a geological or paleontological context, a formation is a group of rock layers.
- **Gnathostome**- A gnathostome is any vertebrate chordate with a moveable jaw (or had an ancestor with one).
- ***Incertae sedis*- A Latin phrase literally meaning "uncertain seat." *"Incertae sedis"* is a term in classification used to refer to a species or group whose relationships with related organisms are unclear or poorly defined.
- **Mesozoic**- An era of time in the Phanerozoic Eon from 249 to 66 million years ago.
- **Mollusk**- Any member of the animal phylum Mollusca, including snails, clams, squid, octopuses, tusk shells and chitons. Most mollusks have a calcium carbonate shell, and a toothed, file-like tongue called a radula. All mollusks have a cape-like organ, the mantle, which usually secretes the shell, and houses breathing organs, and a nervous system.
- **Nekton**- Any aquatic animal that lives either entirely or almost entirely in the water column, and relies on its own swimming or propulsion abilities to keep and move itself in and around the water column. Anchovies, porpoises and ichthyosaurs are examples of nekton.
- **Ordovician**- A period of time in the Paleozoic Era from 484 to 440 million years ago.
- **Paleozoic**- An era of time in the Phanerozoic Eon from 249 to 66 million years ago.
- **Permian**- The last period of time in the Paleozoic Era, the time of "The Great Dying," or most severe of all known extinction events, from 299 to 250 million years ago.

- **Pharynx**- A structure in the throat of many animals located directly behind the mouth or oral chamber. In vertebrates, it often houses breathing structures, like gills.
- **Plankton**- An organism that uses water currents and waterflow to as its primary means of transportation in the water column because it is either too small to move long distances by its own power, or lacks the ability to propel itself entirely. Sargassum seaweed and jellyfish are two varieties of plankton.
- **Pluton**- A geological formation where a body of igneous rock forms through the crystallization of magma slowly cooling far beneath the Earth's surface, and is eventually exposed through geological uplift and erosion.
- **Terrestrial**- Living on land.

Name   Primordial Jawfish

Species	*Entelognathus primordialis*
Phylum	Chordata
Class	Placodermi
Order	? Arthrodira
Size	Holotype is abou 11 centimeters long, living animal may have been over 20 centimeters long
Time Period	Late Ludlow Epoch of the Silurian Period, 419 million years ago
Location	Qujing, Yunnan Province, China
Comments	The Primordial Jawfish, *Entelognathus primordialis*, is the best known of the Silurian-aged placoderms, all of whom are currently known from China. This fame is due to publicity generated over its age, the exquisite preservation of the fossils, and how its anatomy suggests, if not demonstrates a link between arthrodire placoderms and primitive bony fish. This similarity of anatomies is also confirmed with well-preserved skulls of the later-appearing, though more primitive acanthothoracid placoderm, the Canadian Starfacefish, *Romundina stellata*.
	In life, the primordial jawfish had a long, boat-like face with turret-like eyes that were probably immobile. The long mouth may have been used to snap up prey. The stout body is thought to have tapered off into a long, ribbon-like tail, as many, if not most primitive placoderms had very elongated tails.

Name

Tyrant Pitscale Antiarch

Species	*Bothriolepis rex*
Phylum	Chordata
Class	Placodermi
Order	Antiarchi
Family	Bothriolepidae
Size	Known from large fragments: living animal may have been 1.7 meters long.
Time Period	Early Famennian Epoch of the Late Devonian, 370 million years ago.
Location	Nordstrand Point Formation, near Okse Bay, Ellesmere Island, Nunavut, Canada.
Comments	The Tyrant Pitscale Antiarch, *Bothriolepis rex*, is the largest known antiarch placoderm, based on material discovered on Ellesmere Island originally found in 2000. The fragments suggest an animal 1.7 meters long: 30% larger than the now second largest known antiarch, Gross' Giant Pitscale Antiarch, *B. maxima*, from similarly aged marine strata of Latvia, estimated to be 1.4 meters long in comparison. In the picture, however, the tyrant pitscale is compared with the much, much smaller Canadian pitscale, *B. canadensis*, and the blackpan agnathan, *Perscheia pulla*.

The plates of the tyrant pitscale's armor is comparatively very thick compared to other antiarchs. This is thought to be an adaptation for both making the animal negatively buoyant to keep it on or near the substrate, and as defense against predatory sarcopterygian bony fish (related to coelacanths) with "stabbing teeth."

Name	Moroccan Dragonfish
Species	*Draconichthys elegans*
Phylum	Chordata
Class	Placodermi
Order	Arthrodira
Family	Selenosteidae
Size	Skull 11.2 centimeters long, live animal may be up to 100 centimeters long
Time Period	Late Frasnian Epoch of the Late Devonian, 372 million years ago
Location	Nodular limestone horizon of the Kellwasser facies in Lahmida, Rheris Basin, from the Eastern Anti-Atlas Mountains, Morocco
Comments	The Moroccan, or Elegant Dragonfish, *Draconichthys elegans*, is a large selenosteid arthrodire placoderm from the Late Frasnian of Morocco, and lived in a shallow, algae-dimmed sea that covered a region that, today, forms the countries of Germany and Morocco. This algae-dimmed sea would make up a series of geological formations collectively referred to as the "Kellwasser" or "Kellwasserkalk" facies.

The Moroccan dragonfish is named for how its slender skull has, unlike other selenosteids, toothplates with prominent prongs reminescent of the long teeth possessed by modern-day stomiid dragonfishes. Researchers suspect these prominent, tooth-like prongs were used, similar to stomiid teeth, to prevent slippery prey from wriggling out of *D. elegans'* mouth.

The Moroccan dragonfish probably preyed on whatever animal it could catch, including the many other selenosteid placoderms found in the Moroccan reaches of this algae-choked sea, such as (from top) the trio of *Enseosteus marocensis*, *Walterosteus lelieverei*, *Rhinosteus parvus* (in the jaws of the upper dragonfish), or *Driscollaspis pankowskiorum* (between the two dragonfish).

# Name	# Plutonfish
Species	*Denisonodus plutonensis*
Phylum	Chordata
Class	Placodermi
Order	Ptyctodontida
Family	Ptyctodontidae
Size	Head estimated to be about 4 to 5 centimeters long
Time Period	Frasnian Epoch of the Late Devonian, probably 380 to 382 million years ago
Location	Jerome Member of the Martin Formation at Mount Elden, Arizona near the Grand Canyon
Comments	The Plutonfish, *Denisonodus plutonensis*, is a ptyctodontid placoderm, a member of a group of "unarmoured" placoderms who either are descended from arthrodires, or share a common ancestor with arthrodires.

The Plutonfish, *Denisonodus plutonensis*, is a ptyctodontid placoderm, a member of a group of "unarmoured" placoderms who either are descended from arthrodires, or share a common ancestor with arthrodires.

Over the course of their own evolution, ptyctodontids reduced the size of their armor plates. Because of this, most ptyctodontids appear in the fossil record as disarticulated armor fragments and tooth plates. Those few species known from whole-body specimens show animals that look similar to the cartilaginous chimaeras, with long tails and their armor arranged like a hat and neck-brace ensemble.

The plutonfish is named for the presence of a pluton in Mount Elden near where the holotype was found, and the generic name commemorates American palaeoichthyologist Robert Denison, who undertook groundbreaking work to understand placoderms and agnathans, specializing in American species. The plutonfish probably ate shellfish like molluscs and brachiopods.

Name

Panzerfisch

Species	*Hadrosteus rapax*
Phylum	Chordata
Class	Placodermi
Order	Arthrodira
Family	Hadrosteidae
Size	Skull up to 16 centimeters long, living animal may have been 100 to 200 centimeters long
Time Period	Late Frasnian epoch of the Late Devonian period, 372 million years ago
Location	Kellwasserkalk of the *Manticoceras* Beds near Bad Wildungen, Germany
Comments	The Panzerfisch, *Hadrosteus rapax*, is a large arthrodire placoderm, probably about the size of a large trout or a small tuna, from the Kellwasserkalk of Bad Wildungen, in the state of Hesse, Germany.

The panzerfisch shows many similar adaptations to being a visually-based predator in an algae-dimmed sea seen in the unrelated Moroccan dragonfish, including large eyes, and toothplates with fang-like serrations. In this regard, the panzerfisch and the Moroccan dragonfish can be seen as examples of parallel evolution.

Traditionally, the panzerfisch has been seen as a close relative of the terrorfishes of the genera *Dinichthys* and *Dunkleosteus*, and all three genera were housed within the family Dinichthyidae. However, with the recent restriction of Dinichthyidae to *Dinichthys* (and possibly the Chinese terrorfish, *Gannanichthys*), *Hadrosteus* has been placed in its own family, Hadrosteidae together with the mysterious Cleveland Famennian genus, *Diplognathus*.

Name	Geschenkrochen
Species	*Jagorina pandora*
Phylum	Chordata
Class	Placodermi
Order	Rhenanida
Family	Asterosteidae
Size	Skull about 19 centimeters long, body length probably over 100, maybe up to 200 centimeters
Time Period	Late Frasnian epoch of the Late Devonian period, 372 million years ago
Location	Kellwasserkalk of the *Manticoceras* Beds near Bad Wildungen, Germany
Comments	The Gemünden Rochen, *Gemeudina stuertzi*, allows researchers to visualize what rhenanid placoderms looked like in life thanks to its wonderfully preserved fossils. However, because the Gemünden rochen's fossils are squashed flat due to being fossilized in shale that was converted into slate, and because understanding the interrelationships of vertebrates inevitably require an indepth examination of internal anatomy, there are, sadly, limits to what only knowing what an animal looks like can teach people.

In contrast, the Geschenkrochen, or Gift Skate, *Jagorina pandora*, is known from a skull (and parts of the upper body) found in the Kellwasserkalk of Bad Wildungen. Through examination of the geschenkrochen's skull and meager post-cranial remains, palaeoichthyologists now understand that the rhenanids are not primitive placoderms, but are descended from the acanthothoracids, such as the Canadian starfacefish, *Romundina*. Like the Panzerfisch, the geschenkrochen lived in an algae-choked shallow-water sea in what is now Germany. Unlike the panzerfisch, the geschenkrochen lived on the seafloor, and had very small eyes, even when compared to the similar Gemünden rochen. As such, it probably snapped up small animals that it could smell, or sense vibrations from.

Name	Arête Noire
Species	*Melanosteus occitanus*
Phylum	Chordata
Class	Placodermi
Order	Arthrodira
Family	Selenosteidae
Size	Skull about 5 centimeters long, living animal may have been up to 30 centimeters long
Time Period	Late Frasnian epoch of the Late Devonian period, 372 million years ago
Location	Montagne Noire, Occitania, in the south of France
Comments	L'Arête Noire, *Melanosteus occitanus*, is a small to medium-sized selenosteid arthrodire that lived off the coast of the island continet of Armorica during the Late Devonian. By the end of the Devonian, Armorica would fuse with other landmasses that, today, form France, Spain, Morocco, South Africa, South America, Bohemia, Turkey, Iran and the Arabian Peninsula, to form what would become the western reaches of the supercontinent of Gondwana during the early Carboniferous.
	The enormous eyesockets of the arête noire, and its jaws suggest it was a visually-oriented fish-eater. Details of its anatomy suggest that the arête noire is related to selenosteids of the genus *Rhinosteus*.

Name	Rice Turtlefish
Species	*Mizia longhuaensis*
Phylum	Chordata
Class	Placodermi
Order	Antiarchi
Family	Yunnanolepididae
Size	Holotype trunk armor about 2 centimeters wide, long, and tall.
Time Period	Emsian Epoch of the Early Devonian, 393 to 391 million years ago
Location	Xujiachong Formation at Longhua Hill, Qujing, Yunnan Province, China.
Comments	While antiarch placoderms are found throughout the world, one important center of diversity, and probably their place of origin is China. The earliest known fossils of antiarchs are from late Early to Middle Silurian-aged marine strata in China, and demonstrate that antiarchs had already diverged from their acanthothoracid ancestors and were already starting to diversify.

The Rice Turtlefish, *Mizia longhuaensis*, from Early Devonian Qujing, China, is named for how the ridges and depressions on the dorsal side of the trunk armor appear to form the Chinese word "米" ("mi," one of several words for "rice"). The rice turtlefish is a member of the primitive antiarch family Yunnanolepididae, which represents the stage in antiarch evolution where the modified pectoral fin-spine had not yet evolved the elbow-like joint seen in "advanced" antiarchs like the Tyrant pitscale, *B. rex*.

As with all other antiarchs, the rice turtlefish was a sediment-feeder.

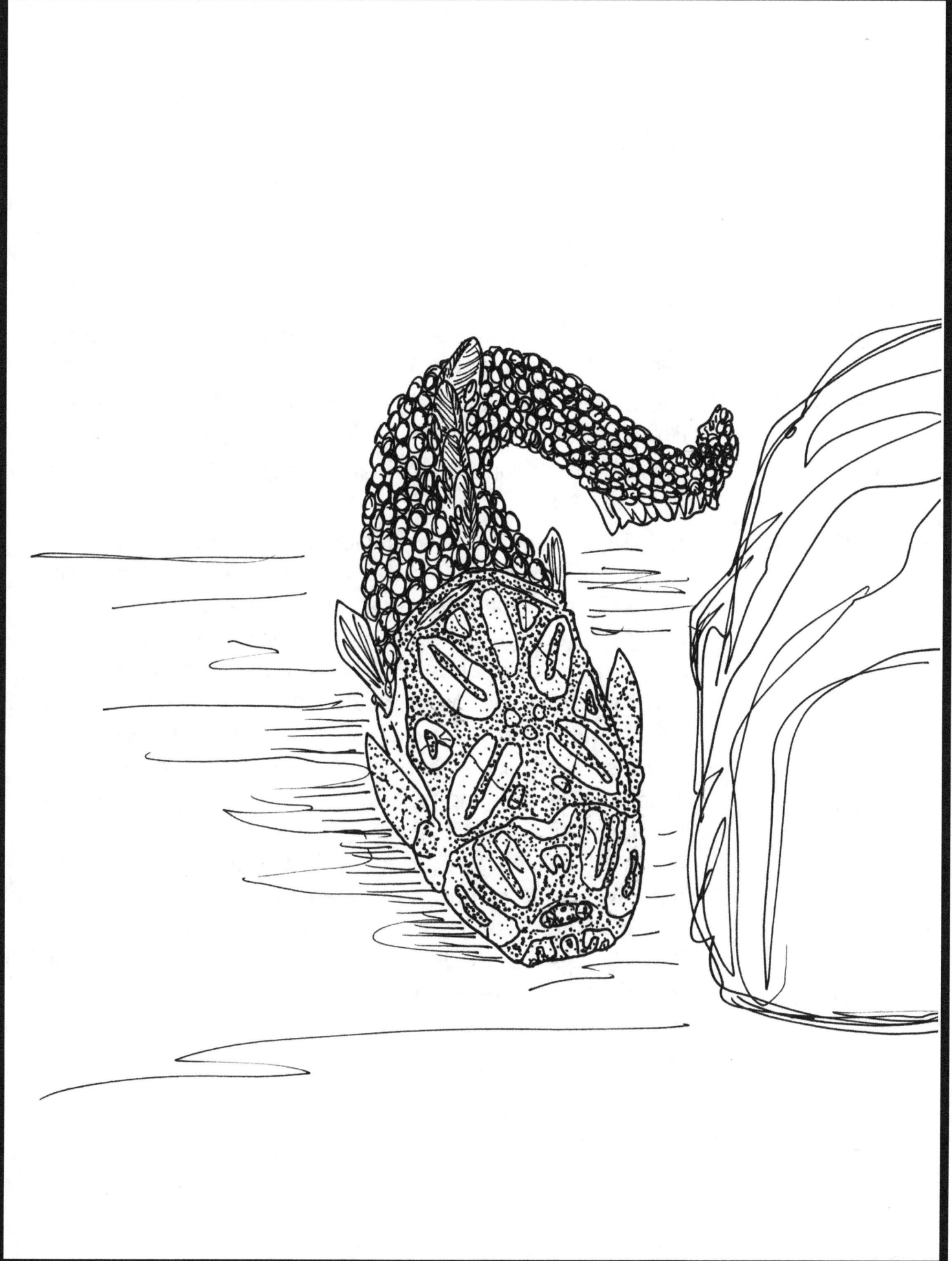

Name	False Titanfish
Species	*Protitanichthys fossatus*
Phylum	Chordata
Class	Placodermi
Order	Arthrodira
Family	Coccosteidae
Size	Skullroof of holotype about 20 centimeters, living animal maybe up to 100 centimeters
Time Period	Eifelian to Lower Givetian Epochs of the Middle Devonian Period, 397 to probably 390 million years ago
Location	Delaware Limestone of Ohio, and Rockport Quarry Michigan, United States
Comments	The False Titanfish, *Protitanichthys fossatus*, is a large coccosteid arthrodire that was originally described from the Eifelian-aged Delaware Limestone formation in Ohio as being a comparatively small progenitor to the Titanfishes of *Titanichthys* from Ohio. Further examinations of the first and successive specimens would show that the animal was not an ancestor of *Titanichthys*, but a relative of *Coccosteus*, and its relatives. There are a few similarities between *Protitanichthys* and arthrodires of the family Plourdeosteidae, too, as well.

A second species, *P. rockportensis*, has been described from the Givetian-aged Rockport Quarry in Michigan, but very little distinguishes it from *P. fossatus*.

Because all coccosteids are thought to be carnivorous, this trio of false titanfishes are shown feeding on a carcass of an antiarch.

Name

Haikou Platefish

Species	*Quasipetalichthys haikouensis*
Phylum	Chordata
Class	Placodermi
Order	Petalichthyida
Family	Quasipetalichthyidae
Size	Skull up to 10 centimeters long
Time Period	Givetian Epoch of the Middle Devonian, 387 to 382 million years ago
Location	Haikou Formation of Kunming, Yunnan Province, China
Comments	The Haikou Platefish, *Quasipetalichthys haikouensis*, is a species of petalichthyid placoderm from Middle Devonian China, and represents a group of primitive petalichthyids who have eyes on the sides of their flattened skulls, rather than near the center-top.

The Haikou Platefish, *Quasipetalichthys haikouensis*, is a species of petalichthyid placoderm from Middle Devonian China, and represents a group of primitive petalichthyids who have eyes on the sides of their flattened skulls, rather than near the center-top.

So far, the Haikou platefish is known from two, poorly preserved skulls from marine strata in the Devonian section of the Haikou Formation, where the skulls were found in association with an antiarch placoderm fauna.

Although its jaws (as well as the jaws of all other petalichthyids) are not known, it is assumed to be a predator that snapped up smaller animals while waiting on the bottom of the seafloor.

Name	# Canadian Starfacefish
Species	*Romundina stellina*
Phylum	Chordata
Class	Placodermi
Order	Acanthothoracida
Family	Palaeacanthanaspidae
Size	Skull about 2 centimeters in length
Time Period	Middle Lochkovian Epoch of the Early Devonian, about 414 to 413 million years ago
Location	Prince of Wales Island, Canada
Comments	

The Canadian Starfacefish, *Romundina stellina*, named in honor of Canadian geologist and paleontologist Dr. Romundur "Ray" Thorsteinsson of Calgary, is one of the best-studied of the acanthothoracid placoderms. The acanthothoracids were a group of heavy-scaled, heavily armored nibblers with large eyes, small, but prominent noses, and large, sharkfin-shaped spines emanating from their thoracic plates.

Reexaminations of skulls of the Canadian starfacefish reaffirms the placement of the acanthothoracids as being the most primitive of placoderms (at least, until paleontologists can find better preserved specimens of the Panzerschimäre, *Stensioella*). Facial and cranial traits seen in the starfacefish are also seen in the Primordial Jawfish, arthrodires, and in more advanced gnathostomates such as humans and tuna.

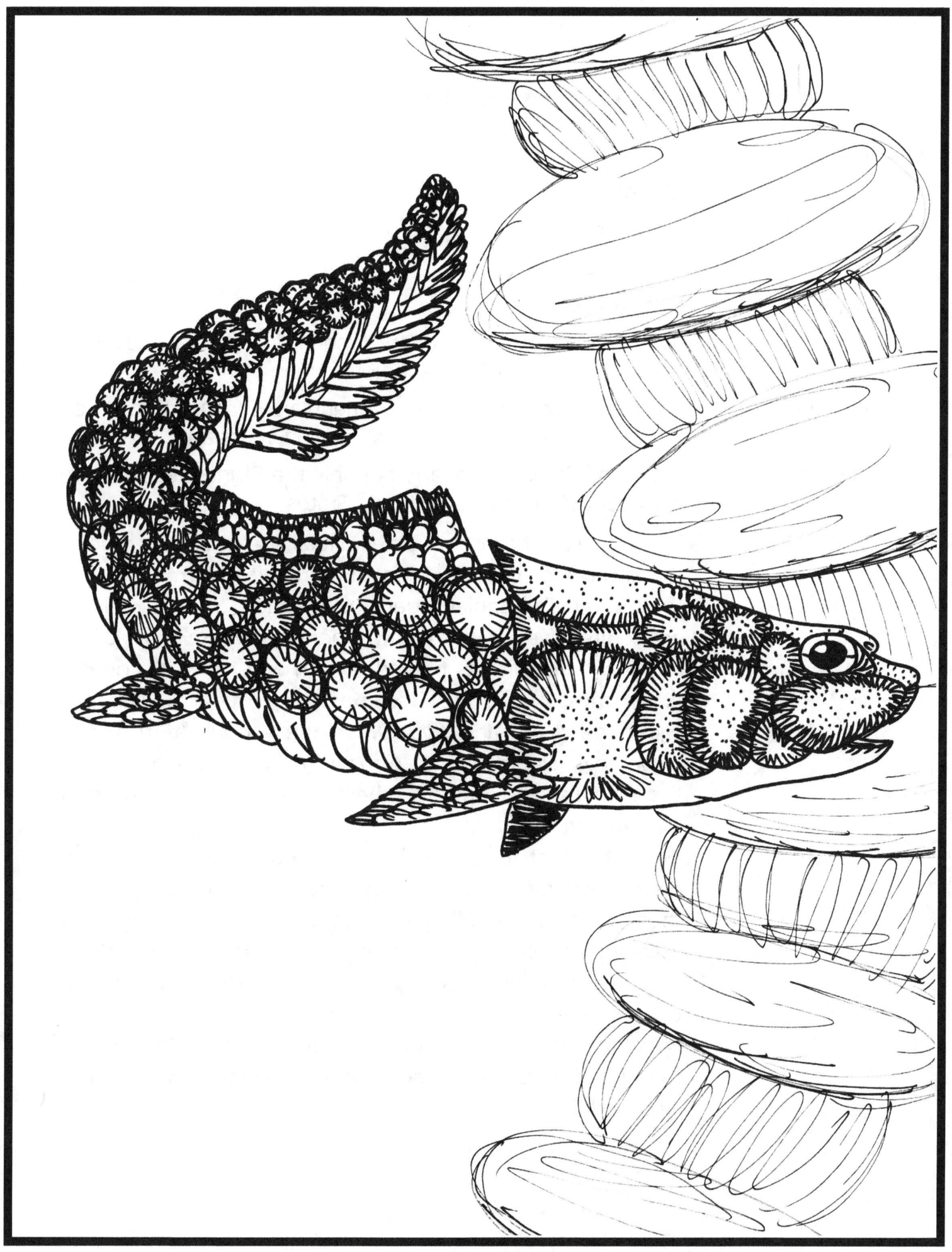

Name	Cleveland Moonfish
Species	*Selenosteus brevis*
Phylum	Chordata
Class	Placodermi
Order	Arthrodira
Family	Selenosteidae
Size	Skull around 16 centimeters long, living animal may have been up to 100 to 150 centimeters long
Time Period	Probably Frasnian to Late Famennian Epochs of the Late Devonian Period, 370ish to 358 million years ago
Location	Cleveland Shale, Ohio, and possibly the Rhinestreet Shale of New York State, Eastern United States.
Comments	The Cleveland Moonfish, *Selenosteus brevis*, is a member of the diverse community of arthrodire placoderms found in the Late Famennian-aged Cleveland Shale. These arthrodires lived in a shallow, open sea where most of the arthrodire inhabitants preyed on fish and other placoderms (i.e., most of the selenosteids like *Selenosteus*, *Gymnotrachelus*, and *Stenosteus*, the various "terrorfishes," *Dinichthys*, *Dunkleosteus*, *Gorgonichthys*, etc.) filterfed (i.e., the titanfishes), or ate shellfish (i.e., the selenosteid *Paramylostoma*).

When the first fossils of the Cleveland moonfish were first discovered and examined, they were originally thought to be those of a very small species of *Titanichthys*, though, this assessment was soon proven to be incorrect when the anatomical differences between *"Titanichthys" brevis* and other species of titanfishes were too profound to ignore.

Fossils of what are probably the Cleveland moonfish are also found in the Frasnian-aged Rhinestreet Shale in what is now New York State.

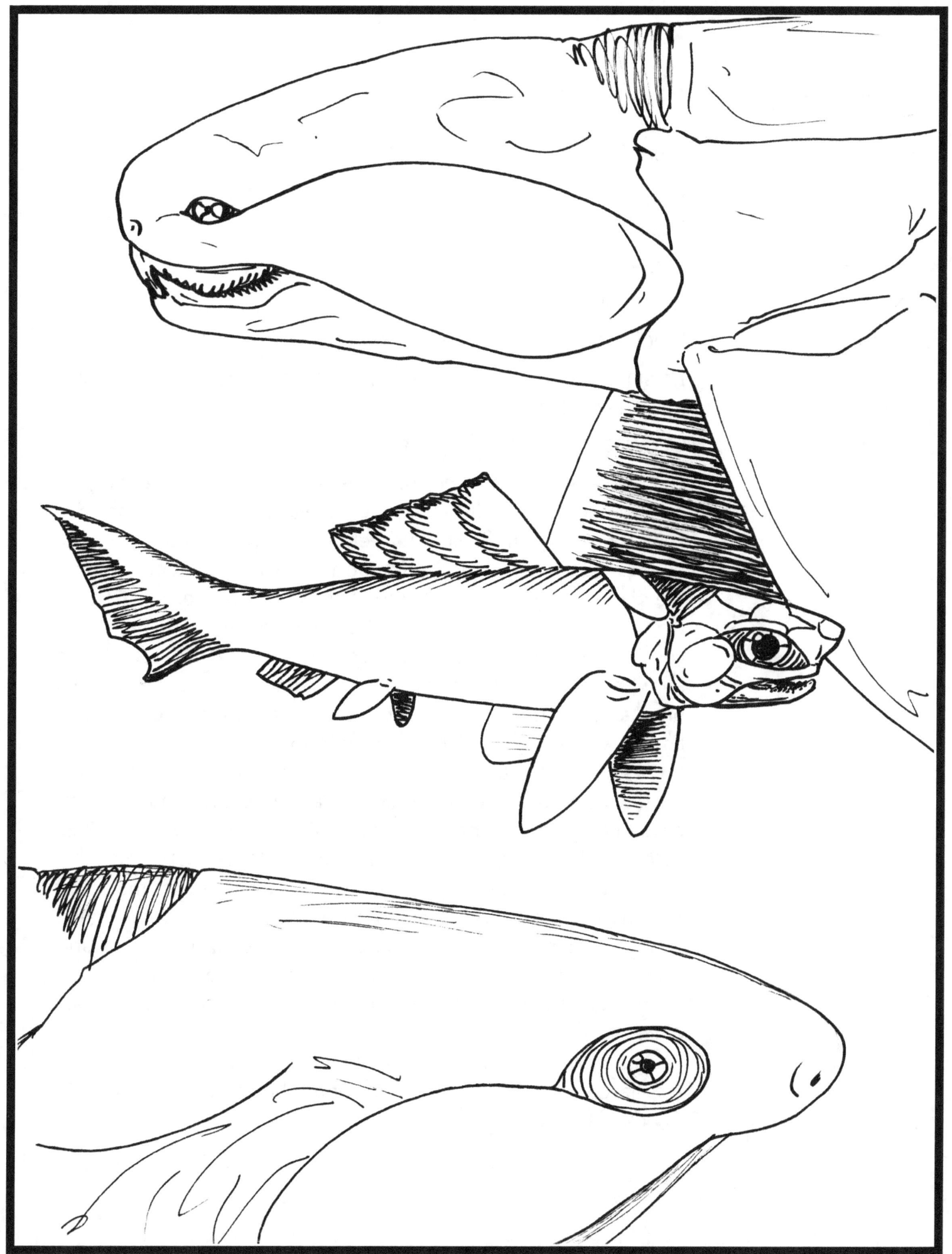

Name	Panzerschimäre
Species	*Stensioella heintzi*
Phylum	Chordata
Class	Placodermi
Order	Stensioellida
Family	Stensioellidae
Size	Holotype is about 26 centimeters long
Time Period	Emsian epoch of the Early Devonian period, 407 to 393 million years ago
Location	Gemünden municipality, Rhein-Hunsrück, Germany
Comments	The Panzerschimäre, *Stensioella heintzi*, of Emsian Germany, is arguably, the most primitive known placoderm, representing a stage in placoderm evolution after the group acquired true jaws, but before the scales of the forebody fused together to become the plates characteristic of (almost) all other placoderm.

Of course, despite lacking plates, the panzerschimäre is still considered a placoderm on account of how its scales are arranged in patterns that blatantly foreshadow the arrangements of plates diagnostic of placoderms, together with skeletal anatomies also diagnostic of placoderms.

Even so, the idea that the panzerschimäre is a placoderm is still the focus of contentious debate. Various palaeoichthyologists have noted that the panzerschimäre physically resembles holocephalid cartilaginous fishes (i.e., chimaeras), and that removing *Stensioella* from taxonomic analyses of the class Placodermi make them synchronize better. On the other hand, there is otherwise very little else that the panzerschimäre and chimaeras proper have in common, and the problem of odd outliers compounding a lack of information are an annoying fact of life.

Because portions of the head decayed before the body was fossilized, it is difficult to understand what sort of lifestyle the living animal had.

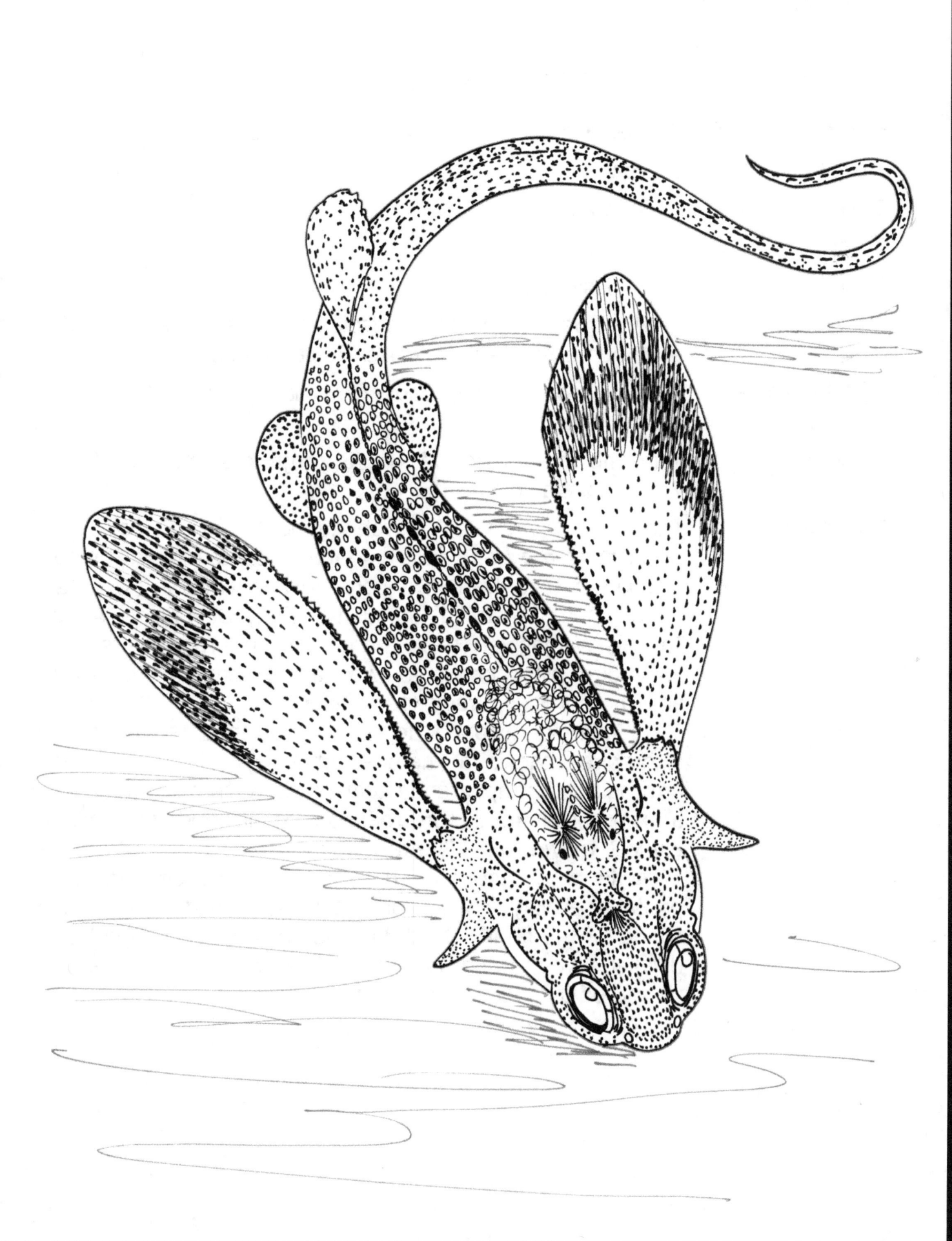

Name	Taemas Wobbegong
Species	*Taemasosteus novaustrocambricus*
Phylum	Chordata
Class	Placodermi
Order	Arthrodira
Family	Buchanosteidae
Size	Known from fragments and isolated plates: head of largest specimen estimated to be over 30 centimeters long.
Time Period	Emsian epoch of the Early Devonian period, 407 to 393 million years ago
Location	Murrumbidgee Series at the Burrinjuck Dam, New South Wales, Australia
Comments	The Taemas Wobbegong, *Taemasosteus novaustrocambricus*, is a large, flattened arthrodire placoderm that lived in a coral reef in what is now New South Wales, Australia, during the Early Devonian. At the Taemas-Weejasper Reef, there was a large diversity of arthrodire placoderms, as well as an endemic family of acanthothoracids, Weejasperaspidae. The Taemas wobbegong is a flattened buchanosteid arthrodire that is a member of a dynasty of flattened arthrodires that apparently culminated with the Homosteids, a group of board-like arthrodires that included some of the earliest known "giant" vertebrates. Lifestyle-wise, though, the Taemas wobbegong was probably ecologically similar to the modern-day wobbegong sharks of the family Orectolobidae, in that it was a bottom-dweller who gobbled up whatever hapless creature wandered too close to its large mouth.

Name

(Louis) Agassiz's Titanfish

Species	*Titanichthys agassizi*
Phylum	Chordata
Class	Placodermi
Order	Arthrodira
Family	Titanichthyidae
Size	Head at least 60 centimeters, living animal may have been 6 meters long
Time Period	Late Famennian Epoch of the Late Devonian Period, 358 million years ago
Location	Cleveland Shale, Ohio.
Comments	The Agassiz's Titanfish, *Titanichthys agassizi*, named after renowned Swiss-American scientist, Louis Agassiz, is a member of a group of enormous, filterfeeding arthrodire placoderms from near the end of the Devonian Period. The titanfishes are probably the largest Devonian vertebrates ever, rivalled in size only by the various terrorfishes (i.e., *Dunkleosteus, Dinichthys, Gorgonichthys*). Unlike the terrorfishes, the titanfishes are thought to have been planktivores, as their mouthplates lacked cutting edges. These otherwise ineffectual mouthplates were thought to, instead, help restrain swallowed plankton, thereby keeping them in the mouth as the water was being expelled. The various species of titanfishes differ from each other by the size, proportions and curvature of the different species' plates.

Name	Wuttagoon Barramundi
Species	*Wuttagoonaspis fletcheri*
Phylum	Chordata
Class	Placodermi
Order	Arthrodira
Family	Wuttagoonaspididae
Size	Head up to 18 centimeters long, adults may probably be up to 100 centimeters long
Time Period	Givetian Epoch of the Middle Devonian, 390 million years ago
Location	Georgina Basin of western Queensland, Australia.
Comments	The Wuttagoon Barramundi, *Wuttagoonaspis fletcheri*, is a primitive arthrodire from Middle Devonian Queensland, Australia. It is known from numerous fossil specimens of both adults and juveniles. Like other primitive arthrodires, and unlike more advanced arthrodires, the Wuttagoon barramundi had a very scaly body covered in thick, multi-layered, sculptured scales. The skull and armor are also covered in ornamentation that changed as the animal matured: in juveniles, the ornamentation consisted of tubercles arranged either randomnly, or in rows, which then changed to mostly parallel, concentric rows, with some tubercles. The Wuttagoon barramundi's closest relatives, outside of other wuttagoonaspids like the Milligan's barramundi, *W. milligani*, and the Whatfish, *Yiminaspis*, are the actinolepids, and possibly the phyllolepids.

Name	Perfume Trout
Species	*Xiangshuiosteus*
Phylum	Chordata
Class	Placodermi
Order	Arthrodira
Suborder	Brachythoraci
Family	?Dunkleosteidae
Size	Holotype and only known specimen suggests a skull at least 5 to 5.5 centimeters long.
Time Period	Late Emsian Epoch of the Early Devonian, about 397 million years ago.
Location	Near Xiangshui Valley, Jiucheng Formation, Wuding of Yunnan Province, China.
Comments	The Perfume Trout, *Xiangshuiosteus wui*, is a peculiar arthrodire placoderm so far known only from a flattened skull roof reminiscent of a Buddhist cap. The generic and common names refers to Xiangshui Valley, " 香水穀 near the region where the holotype specimen was found. When the specimen was first studied in 1992, it was thought to be a transitional form between buchanosteids and coccosteids. A later study in 2013, however places the perfume trout in Dunkleosteidae as a close relative of the Australian Sea Boar, *Eastmanosteus calliaspis*, from the Late Frasnian-aged Gogo Reef, and no longer a transitional form. The Late Emsian-aged Jiucheng Formation had an extensive community of placoderms, including several additional arthrodires and tiny antiarchs.

Bibliography

- Anderson, P.S.L.; Westneat, M. (2009). "A biomechanical model of feeding kinematics for Dunkleosteus terrelli (Arthrodira, Placodermi)". *Paleobiology*. **35** (2): 251–269

- Carr, Robert Keegan. *Placoderm systematics, diversity, and evolution*. Diss. 1994.

- CARR, ROBERT K.; GARY L. JACKSON (2005). "*DIPLOGNATHUS LAFARGEI* SP. NOV. FROM THE ANTRIM SHALE (UPPER DEVONIAN) OF THE MICHIGAN BASIN, MICHIGAN, USA" Revista Brasileira de Paleontologia. 8 (2): 019–116 (113)

- Denison, Robert (1978). *Placodermi* Volume 2 of Handbook of Paleoichthyology. Stuttgart New York: Gustav Fischer Verlag. p. 105. ISBN 978-0-89574-027-4.

- Denison, Robert H. "Further consideration of placoderm evolution." *Journal of Vertebrate Paleontology* (1983): 69-83.

- Downs, Jason P., et al. "A new large-bodied species of *Bothriolepis* (Antiarchi) from the Upper Devonian of Ellesmere Island, Nunavut, Canada." *Journal of Vertebrate Paleontology* 36.6 (2016): e1221833.

- Dupret, Vincent, et al. "The internal cranial anatomy of Romundina stellina Ørvig, 1975 (Vertebrata, Placodermi, Acanthothoraci) and the origin of jawed vertebrates—Anatomical atlas of a primitive gnathostome." *PloS one* 12.2 (2017): e0171241.

- Dupret, Vincent. "A new wuttagoonaspid (Placodermi, Arthrodira) from the Lower Devonian of Yunnan (South China): origin, dispersal, and paleobiogeographic significance." *Journal of Vertebrate Paleontology* 28.1 (2008): 12-20.

- Friedman, Matt; Martin D. Brazeau (2013). "News & Views: Palaeontology: A jaw-dropping fossil fish". *Nature*. **502**: 175–177.

- Hussakof, L. "V.—Notes on some Upper Devonian Arthrodira from Ohio, USA, in the British Museum (Natural History)." *Geological Magazine (Decade V)* 8.03 (1911): 123-128.

- Janvier, Philippe. "Early Vertebrates" Oxford, New York: Oxford University Press, 1998. ISBN 0-19-854047-7

- Jiang, Pan. "Devonian Vertebrates from Old Red Sandstone Facies in China." (1988): 609-618.

- Johnson, Heidemarie G., and David K. Elliott. "A new ptyctodont (Placodermi) from the Upper Devonian Martin Formation of northern Arizona, and an analysis of ptyctodont phylogeny." *Journal of Paleontology* 70.06 (1996): 994-1003.

- LELIÉVRE, H.; FEIST, R.; GOUJET, D.; BLIECK, A. (1987). "Les vertébrés de la Montagne Noire (Sud de la France) et leur apport á la phylogénie des Pachyostéomorphes (Placodermes, Arthrodires).". *Palaeovertebrata*. **17**: 1–16.

- Long, John A. The Rise of Fishes: 500 Million Years of Evolution Baltimore: The Johns Hopkins University Press, 1996. ISBN 0-8018-5438-5

- Long, John A. (1993). Palaeozoic vertebrate biostratigraphy and biogeography. 156: Johns Hopkins University Press, 1993. p. 369. ISBN 9780801847790.

- Miles, Roger S. "Protitanichthys and some other coccosteomorph arthrodires from the

Devonian of North America." (1966).

- Pradel, Alan, et al. "An enigmatic gnathostome vertebrate skull from the Middle Devonian of Bolivia." *Acta Zoologica* 90.s1 (2009): 123-133.
- Ritchie, Alexander. "Wuttagoonaspis gen. nov., an unusual arthrodire from the Devonian of Western New South Wales, Australia." *Palaeontographica Abteilung A* (1973): 58-72.
- Rücklin, Martin. "First selenosteid placoderms from the eastern Anti-Atlas of Morocco; osteology, phylogeny and palaeogeographical implications." *Palaeontology* 54.1 (2011): 25-62.
- Rücklin, Martin, John A. Long, and Kate Trinajstic. "A new selenosteid arthrodire ('Placodermi') from the Late Devonian of Morocco." *Journal of Vertebrate Paleontology* 35.2 (2015): e908896.
- VAŠKANINOVÁ, VALÉRIA, and Petr Kraft. "The largest Lower Devonian placoderm-Antineosteus rufus sp. nov. from the Barrandian area (Czech Republic)." *Bulletin of Geosciences* 89.3 (2014).
- Wang, Junqing (April 1992). "NEW DISCOVERY OF EARLY MIDDLE DEVONIAN BRACHY-THORACID (PLACODERM FISH) FROM WUDING REGION OF YUNNAN". *Vertebrata PalAsiatica*. **30** (2): 111–119.
- Wang, Junqing, and Zhu Min. "Age of the Jiucheng Formation of Wuding, Yunnan [J]." *JOURNAL OF STRATIGRAPHY* 1 (1995).
- White, Errol. *Australian arthrodires*. British Museum (Natural History), 1952.
- White, Errol I. "The larger arthrodiran fishes from the area of the Burrinjuck Dam, NSW." *The Transactions of the Zoological Society of London* 34.2 (1978): 149-262.
- Zhu, Min. (1996). "The Phylogeny of Antiarcha (Placodermi, Pisces), with the Description of Early Devonian Antiarchs from Qujing, Yunnan, China." *Bulletin du Muséum national d'Histoire naturelle*. **18**: 233–347.
- Zhu, Min; Yu, Xiaobo; Ahlberg, Per Erik; Choo, Brian; Lu, Jing; Qiao, Tuo; Qu, Qingming; Zhao, Wenjin; Jia, Liantao; Blom, Henning; Zhu, You'an (2013). "A Silurian placoderm with osteichthyan-like marginal jaw bones". *Nature*. **502**: 188–193.
- Zhu, You-An, and Min Zhu. "A redescription of *Kiangyousteus yohii* (Arthrodira: Eubrachythoraci) from the Middle Devonian of China, with remarks on the systematics of the Eubrachythoraci." Zoological Journal of the Linnean Society169.4 (2013): 798-819.

About the Artist

Stanton F. Fink is a student of Biology and Chinese Medicine, and makes a hobby of drawing monsters and researching flowers, arcane-looking creatures, prehistoric animals, fish, reptiles, birds and the occasional, really grotesque fungal fruiting body.

Stanton grew up and went to school in California and is currently living, drawing, and gardening in Oregon.

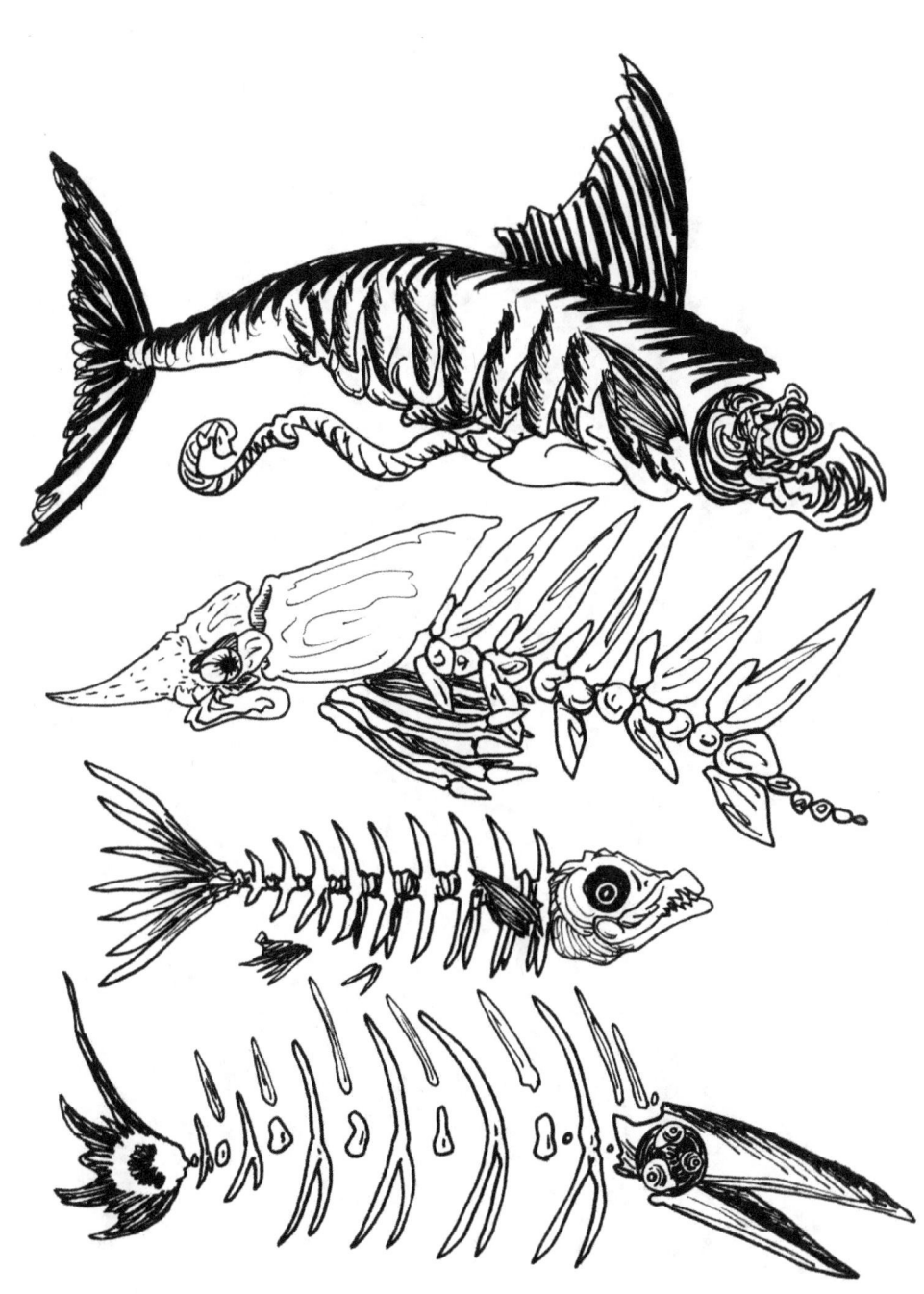